THE
ROCK
Foundation of All Life

by
Nancy M. Femenella
Illustrated by
Lesley-Anne Dale

I thank my God and my husband, Art Sr.,
without which my life would be a hollow vessel.
I would like to thank Lesley-Anne Dale, my illustrator, for her creations,
her patience and her perseverance. She made my words come alive.
I would like to thank my friend Lori Serra for her encouragement over several years,
To write and to publish.
The love I have for our children, and their families,
motivates me to encourage other parents
To find moments each day to teach our children to pray.

Let us grow together in His grace.
With God's love,
Nancy

The **Rock**
upon which,

Birds
rest
and build
their nest.

Small fish
gather 'round
The **Rock**…
Huddling together
in a school,
a hideaway…
Hoping not
to be seen by
big
hungry mouths.

Seals climb up and down… And into the sea.

A place and time to sunbathe,

To give birth to their young.

The kelp attaches
to the **Rock**;

In the water,
sea otters twirl about;
Wrapping themselves
like a package
in the kelp…
no doubt.

Sometimes, they hold hands
        as they sleep,

So as not to drift away
              into the deep.

In a pouch
under their left arm,
They hide a stone;

Which they use as a tool
to hammer open

abalone.

Starfish and mussels
attach themselves to
rocks.

The rocks
are where the sand,
seeds and water
are caught
By the churning sea.....

Aha!
A Beach!

A Beach is made.

In the shallows, clams
can bury themselves;

And conchs find space
    to walk;
They sift the sand
    searching
for bits of food.

Meanwhile…

Sweeping stingrays
forage for shrimp;

Overhead,
the Monarch Butterfly
Flies and flies…
Onward for miles and miles.

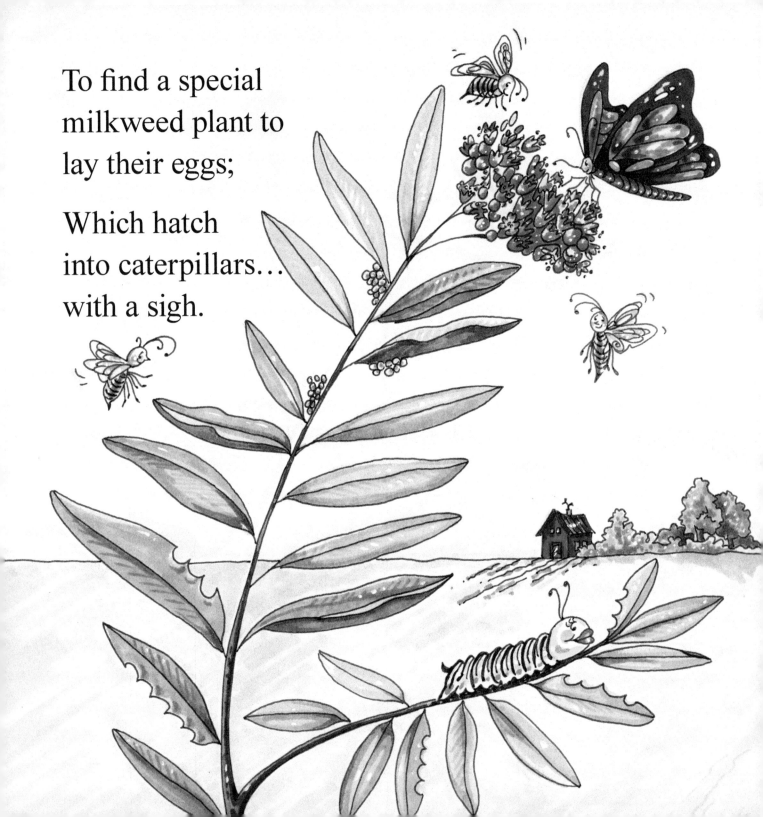

To find a special
milkweed plant to
lay their eggs;

Which hatch
into caterpillars…
with a sigh.

The caterpillars
eat the milkweed;

Then hang upside
down, making a chrysalis.

Emerging....before long
into a beautiful Monarch Butterfly!

There on the beach, a man and woman walk
and their children play;

Building sand castles
and playing catch;
All want to stay.....

The family relaxes as daytime comes to an end...
Watching as the sun sets;

And day becomes night.

Only to visit...
Another time,

Another day...

They might?

Sandpipers
and gulls stand alone
at water's edge;
Wave after wave
pounding
the sand;

And

The **ROCK**…..
The **ROCK**,
upon which we stand,
is our **God**!
We build our life upon
THE ROCK…

The Creator of all!

The sky above,

And...below

the endless oceans we see...

The stars, The Moon, All creatures, you know.

We thank HIM for all,
The **ROCK**
          and the sea;
The stars
          And the moon,

You,
And little Ol' me.

Can You Find?

- Shrimp
- Sea Otter
- Sting Ray
- Angelfish
- Octopus
- Sea Urchin
- Starfish
- Flying Fish
- Sea Turtle
- Brittlestar
- Crab
- Hermit Crab
- Atlantic Wing Oyster
- Periwinkle
- Queen Conch
- Reef Squid
- Flamingo Tongue
- Christmas Tree Worm
- Limpet
- Comb Jellies
- Anemone
- Brain Coral
- Elkhorn Coral
- Puffer Fish
- Butterfly Fish
- Staghorn Coral
- Rock

- Angel Fish
- Whale
- Dolphin
- Manta Ray
- Moray Eel
- Monarch Butterfly
- Clams
- Seahorse
- Pipefish
- Spiny Lobster
- Sea Gull
- Sand Piper
- Bee
- Mermaids Purse
- Snail
- Shell
- Jelly Fish
- Mussels
- Feather Duster Worm
- Seaweed
- Sand Dollar
- Abalone
- Caterpillar
- Chrysalis
- Moon
- Stars
- Seeds

WestBow Press books may be ordered through booksellers or by contacting:

WestBow Press
A Division of Thomas Nelson & Zondervan
1663 Liberty Drive
Bloomington, IN 47403
www.westbowpress.com
1 (866) 928-1240

ISBN: 978-1-5127-5241-0 (sc)
ISBN: 978-1-5127-5240-3 (e)

Library of Congress Control Number: 2016912860

Print information available on the last page.

WestBow Press rev. date: 08/19/2016

WESTBOW
PRESS*
A DIVISION OF THOMAS NELSON
& ZONDERVAN

CPSIA information can be obtained
at www.ICGtesting.com
Printed in the USA
BVOW07s1822090916

461606BV00003B/4/P